Investigate Science

What's the Weather?

by Melissa Stewart

Content Adviser: Jan Jenner, Ph.D.

Science Adviser: Terrence E. Young Jr., M.Ed., M.L.S., Jefferson Parish (La.) Public Schools

Reading Adviser: Rosemary G. Palmer, Ph.D., Department of Literacy, College of Education, Boise State University

COMPASS POINT BOOKS MINNEAPOLIS, MINNESOTA

Compass Point Books
3109 West 50th St., #115
Minneapolis, MN 55410

Visit Compass Point Books on the Internet at *www.compasspointbooks.com* or e-mail your request to *custserv@compasspointbooks.com*

Photographs ©: Gary Sundermeyer, cover (middle); Charles Mauzy/Corbis, cover background, 1; Corbis, 4 (top), 25; DigitalVision, 4 (bottom); Richard Hutchings/Corbis, 5; PhotoDisc, 7 (all), 10 (all), 23; Daniel Hodges, 8 (all); Daniel Johnson, 11; Corel, 12; Gregg Andersen, 13, 15 (all), 24 (all); Ken McGraw/Index Stock Imagery, 14; Photri-Microstock/Lani Howe, 16; Ed Bock/Corbis, 17; Bill Schild/Corbis, 18 (top); Gary W. Carter/Corbis, 18 (bottom); B. and C. Gillingham/Index Stock Imagery, 19; Richard Walters/Visuals Unlimited, 20; Matthias Kulka/Corbis, 21; DPA/Dembinsky Photo Associates, 22.

Creative Director: Terri Foley
Managing Editor: Catherine Neitge
Editors: Nadia Higgins, Christianne C. Jones
Photo Researcher: Svetlana Zhurkina
Designer: The Design Lab
Illustrator: Jeffrey Scherer
Educational Consultant: Diane Smolinski

Library of Congress Cataloging-in-Publication Data
Stewart, Melissa.
What's the weather? / by Melissa Stewart.
  p. cm. — (Investigate science)
Summary: Introduces different types of weather and precipitation through text, illustrations, and activities.
Includes bibliographical references and index.
ISBN 0-7565-0639-5 (hardcover)
1. Weather—Juvenile literature. [1. Weather.] I. Title. II. Series.
QC981.3.S74 2004
551.6—dc22   2003022719

Note to Readers: There are many ways to learn about the weather. One way is to watch the sky and look for patterns. By writing and drawing everything they notice, scientists can often predict weather changes.

This book will help you study weather the way a scientist does. To get started, you will need a notebook and a pencil.

In the Doing More section in the back of the book, you will find step-by-step instructions for some more fun science experiments and activities.

In this book, words that are defined in the glossary are in **bold** the first time they appear in the text.

Table of Contents

As you read this book, be on the lookout for these special symbols:

 Ask an adult for help.

 Turn to the back of the book for another activity.

 Go to page 30 for an explanation to a question.

Weather Every Day

Go outside and feel the air. Look up at the sky and down at the ground. Is it sunny or cloudy? Rainy or windy? Hot or cold? What's the weather?

Think about how much the weather affects your life. It determines what clothes you wear and how much time you can spend outdoors. Have you ever had to stay home from school because of too much snow? Have you ever lost electricity during a big storm?

Scientists who study the weather are called **meteorologists.** We depend a lot on meteorologists to give us accurate weather reports. Let's do some experiments with weather and come up with our own reports!

Big storms can cause major power outages.

The weather
affects what
you wear and
how you play.

Keep Track of Weather Changes

The weather is always changing. To keep track of weather changes, get a calendar with a separate page for each month. If it is sunny, draw a picture of the sun on that day. If it is cloudy, draw a **cloud.** Think of ways to show it is raining, snowing, or windy. Come up with ways to mark the calendar if the weather changes during the day. Use a thermometer to measure the temperature outside. Record that on your calendar, too.

At the end of each month, count the number of days with each kind of weather. Compare your results for several months. Which month had the most sunny days? The most windy days? The most rainy days?

Think About It!

What's the difference between weather and climate? See page 30 for an answer.

? See Explanation

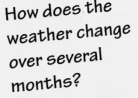
How does the weather change over several months?

Compare the temperature at different times during the day.

Notice Temperature Changes During a Day

You can also observe how the weather changes during a single day. For three days, look at an outdoor thermometer when you wake up, when you get home from school, and at bedtime. Make a chart like the one pictured here. Do you notice any patterns in the temperature? At what time of day is it warmest? When is it coolest? Can you explain the reason for these patterns? See page 30 for an answer.

?
See Explanation

What you need:
• *an outdoor thermometer*

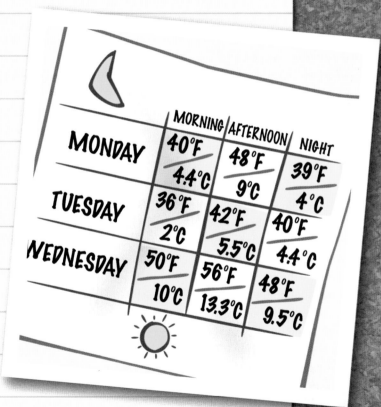

	MORNING	AFTERNOON	NIGHT
MONDAY	40°F / 4.4°C	48°F / 9°C	39°F / 4°C
TUESDAY	36°F / 2°C	42°F / 5.5°C	40°F / 4.4°C
WEDNESDAY	50°F / 10°C	56°F / 13.3°C	48°F / 9.5°C

Clouds, Rain, and Snow

Examine Clouds

Look up at the sky and draw a picture of the clouds you see. Are they high and thin or low and thick? Are they white and puffy or dark and flat?

Draw pictures of the clouds every day for a week. Write what the weather was like under each of the drawings. Can you see any connection between what clouds look like and a type of weather? In your notebook, record your conclusions about the connection.

Most of the time, thick dark clouds mean rain is on the way. Puffy white clouds mean the weather is good. Thin wispy clouds mean the weather is about to change for better or for worse.

Notice how clouds change throughout a week.

Did You Know?

Before there was TV or radio, many people used the clouds to predict the weather.

Did You Know?

Fog is a cloud that touches the ground. Fog often forms near the sea. When warm, moist air above the water's surface drifts over cold land, fog appears. It breaks up when the land warms up.

See a Cloud Close Up

To see a cloud close up, open the door of your freezer and observe what happens. After a few seconds, does it look cloudy inside? Now blow into the freezer a few times. What happens? (If you don't see results, try this the next time you are at the grocery store, where the freezers are colder.)

What you need:
• a very cold freezer

The air in your kitchen is warm, just like the air near the ground outside. Warm air is full of an invisible **gas** called **water vapor.** The air in your freezer is cold, just like the air where clouds form. When warm air meets cold air, the water vapor in the warm air cools. It changes into tiny water droplets you can see. Clouds are made of these tiny water droplets.

Blow into a freezer to make a cloud.

For another activity about clouds, turn to page 26.

13

Rain falls when drops of water in a cloud become heavy enough.

See How Raindrops Form

The water droplets inside a cloud move around a lot. They crash and clump together to form bigger, heavier drops. You can see how water acts inside a cloud. Using a medicine dropper, place several drops of water on a piece of waxed paper. Pick up the paper and tilt it gently. What happens when the drops touch?

When the drops of water in a cloud become heavy enough, they fall to the ground as rain. If it is cold enough, it snows.

See page 27 for another activity about rain.

What you need:
• a medicine dropper
• water
• waxed paper

See how water droplets bump and stick together as they do in a cloud.

Doing More

15

Examine Rain

The next time it rains, put on a raincoat and go outside. Use your senses to observe everything you can about the rain.

- How large are the drops?

- What sounds does rain make?

- Does the rain have a smell? (Rain can be polluted, so don't taste it.)

- How does it feel?

- What happens to the rain when it hits the sidewalk, a garden, or a lawn?

Record all your observations in your notebook.

Notice what happens to rain once it hits the ground.

It can be fun to explore outside on a rainy day.

Look for all the places puddles form.

Observe Puddles

When the rain stops, look for puddles. Where do they form?

See Explanation

Can you explain why?

Sometimes, after a rainy morning, the sun will come out. When this happens, go outside and look for a shallow puddle on a driveway or on a sidewalk. Use chalk to draw a line around the puddle. Draw a new line around the puddle every 30 minutes. What is happening to the puddle?

See Explanation

Why? See page 30 for an answer.

What you need:
• a puddle
• a piece of chalk

Notice how a puddle changes after the sun comes out.

19

Compare Snowflakes

If you live in a place where it snows, you can see something pretty amazing. The next time you spot flakes falling, grab some black construction paper and a magnifying glass. Also grab some plain paper and a pencil for drawing, and head outside.

Hold the black paper out to catch some snowflakes. Look closely at the flakes with the magnifying glass. Draw the snowflakes in as much detail as you can. How are all the snowflakes similar? How are they different? Write your conclusions in your notebook.

Catch a snowflake, and draw it as carefully as you can.

If you look closely, you can see differences among snowflakes.

How Wind Works

When the sun heats air that is near the ground, that air expands. As it spreads out, the air becomes lighter and rises higher in the sky. Cool air rushes down to take its place. The moving air is what we call wind.

You can't see wind, but you can feel it. You can hear it flutter leaves or watch it push clouds across the sky. Wind can be very powerful.

On a windy day, go outside and look for signs of wind at work. Draw pictures of three things wind can do.

Did You Know?

Over time, wind can wear away or reshape the land. This process is called **erosion.**

22

Wind is powerful enough to push a sailboat across a lake.

Use a wind stick to find the windiest places in your yard.

24

Make a Wind Stick

Some places are windier than others—even in your own yard. To find out why, make a wind stick. Use packing tape to attach a plastic garbage bag to one end of a long stick, such as a broom handle. Cut the garbage bag into long strips. Hold the stick out in front of you and slowly walk around your yard. Where do the strips move the most? Where do they move the least?

Make lists of everything you see around the spots where the strips blow the most and where they blow the least. Why do you think some areas are windier than others? See page 30 for an answer. For another activity using your wind stick, see page 28.

See Explanation

Doing More

Now that you have studied the weather, you are thinking like a meteorologist. What else do you notice about the sun, clouds, rain, snow, and wind? What other types of weather happen where you live?

See page 30 for an answer. For another activity using your wind stick, see page 28.

What you need:
• packing tape
• a plastic garbage bag
• a long, sturdy stick
• scissors

What kinds of weather have you experienced?

How Do Clouds Form?

On page 13, you learned an easy way to see a cloud in your freezer. To see how clouds form naturally, try this experiment.

What you need:
- a spoon
- a little bit of soil and grass
- a resealable plastic bag
- water
- tape

1. Go outside and collect 3 spoonfuls of soil and a little bit of grass.

2. Place the soil and grass at the bottom of a small, resealable plastic bag.

3. Add 1 spoonful of water to the soil. Be careful not to get the sides of the bag wet.

4. Seal the bag and tape it to a sunny window. Observe the bag after 5, 10, and 15 minutes. What do you see? What happens when you tap the sides of the bag?

Measure Rainfall

On page 15, you learned how tiny water droplets join together and fall as rain. To measure how much rain falls in a single storm, try this activity.

1. Thoroughly clean a large, plastic jar, such as a peanut butter jar.

Ask an Adult

2. Ask an adult to cut a large plastic soda bottle in half.

3. Turn the top half of the bottle upside down and place it inside the jar. The soda-bottle funnel will catch raindrops.

4. Now use a ruler and a permanent marker to mark $1/2$-inch (1.3-centimeter) divisions along the side of the jar.

5. Place the jar in an open area outdoors. After the next rainfall, check the jar to see how much rain fell.

See Explanation

6. In the winter, you can use the jar to measure snowfall. After a snowstorm, take the jar inside and wait for the snow to melt. Predict whether the water level will be greater than, less than, or equal to the snow level. Were you right?

What you need:
- a wind stick (from page 25)
- 4 rocks
- a permanent marker
- a hammer

Find the Wind's Direction

On page 25, you used a wind stick to find the places in your yard that are the most and least windy. You can also use your wind stick to find out which direction the wind is blowing. The instructions below will show you how.

Ask an Adult

1. Ask an adult to help you figure out whether your house faces north, south, east, or west. Then figure out where the three other directions are. (Here's a tip: In the morning, the sun will be in the east. In the afternoon, it moves toward the west.)

2. Find four good-sized rocks that look different from each other. Each rock will serve as a marker for each of the four directions. Use a permanent marker to label the rocks N (north), E (east), S (south), and W (west).

3. Find a windy spot outside where you would like to test the direction of the wind. Arrange your markers here. Imagine there's a compass on the ground. The rock that stands for north is straight north of the one that represents south. East and west are opposite each other going the other direction.

Ask an Adult

4. With an adult's help, use a hammer to pound your wind stick in the middle of the four markers.

For the next week, watch the wind stick closely. Which day is the windiest? What direction does the wind most often blow from—north, south, east, or west? (Remember that the wind is blowing from the opposite direction that the plastic strips flutter.) Write down your results in a notebook.

Explanations to Questions

Weather and Climate
(from Think About It! page 6)
Weather refers to what it's like outside during one day, or for even a couple of hours or minutes. The weather can vary within a small area. Climate has to do with what the weather is usually like. Climate also covers wide areas. So, for example, even though Arizona has a dry, desert climate, the weather can still be rainy from time to time.

Changing Temperatures *(from page 9)*
It's warmest in the middle of the day, between 1 and 3 p.m. The sun has been slowly warming the land and air all day. After this time, the sun sinks lower in the western sky, and its power decreases.

Where Puddles Form *(from page 19)*
Puddles form in dips and low spots in the sidewalk and the lawn. Imagine if you spilled a glass of water on a ramp. You know that water travels from higher places to lower places.

Disappearing Puddles *(from page 19)*
When the water in a puddle heats up, it evaporates. It changes into a gas called water vapor. The vapor rises into the sky, and the puddle gets smaller and smaller.

Windy Areas *(from page 25)*
Wind can be blocked by houses, fences, trees, and other big objects. Open areas will be windiest because there are fewer things blocking the wind.

Melting Snow *(from page 27)*
Snow is fluffy. It takes up more room in the jar than it does when it melts into water.

Glossary

climate—the way weather usually is in a certain area

cloud—a group of millions of tiny water droplets or ice crystals in the sky; clouds form when water vapor in the air cools down and changes from a gas to a liquid

erosion—the breaking up or wearing away of land

fog—a cloud that touches land

gas—a substance like air that spreads to fill any space; most gases are invisible

meteorologists—scientists who study the weather

water vapor—water that has turned into a gas; the air contains water vapor

To Find Out More

At the Library

DiSpezio, Michael A. *Weather Mania: Discovering What's Up and What's Coming Down*. New York: Sterling Publishing, 2002.

Root, Phyllis. *One Windy Wednesday*. Cambridge, Mass.: Candlewick Press, 1996.

Sherman, Josepha. *Sunshine: A Book About Sunlight*. Minneapolis: Picture Window Books, 2004.

On the Web

For more information on weather, use FactHound to track down Web sites related to this book.

1. Go to *www.facthound.com*
2. Type in a search word related to this book or this book ID: 0756506395.
3. Click on the *Fetch It* button.

Your trusty FactHound will fetch the best Web sites for you!

Index

About the Author

Melissa Stewart earned a bachelor's degree in biology from Union College and a master's degree in science and environmental journalism from New York University. After editing children's science books for nearly a decade, she decided to focus on writing. She has written more than 50 science books for children and contributed articles to *ChemMatters*, *Instructor*, *MATH*, *National Geographic World*, *Natural New England*, *Odyssey*, *Ranger Rick*, *Science World*, and *Wild Outdoor World*. She also teaches writing workshops and develops hands-on science programs for schools near her home in Northborough, Massachusetts.